Poetic Reflections

The Patterns of Life

VitaGold

Poetic Reflections – The Paterns of Life © 2017 by
VitaGold

.

For information contact: info@uptownmediaventures.com

Book and Cover design by Team Uptown

ISBN: 978-1-68121-087-2

First Edition: November 2017

Sankofa
Freedom Press

10 9 8 7 6 5 4 3 2 1

Dedicated to my dad and the poets of Cleveland who have inspired me over the years.

Table of Contents

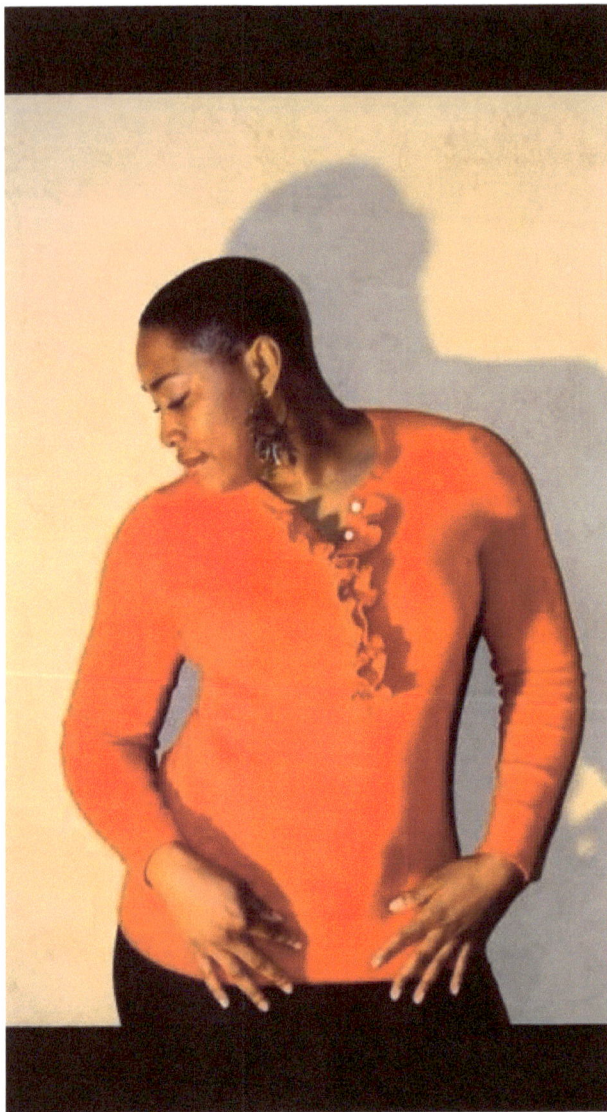

A Walk Outside

Today I walked outside with no umbrella because the rain hasn't fallen in a while and my tears have been locked up so I took this moment to shed a few.
I let the showers cleanse my soul it was as if in this moment Jehovah was washing away all the stress and anxiety of this world.
Yes it rains upon sinner and saint alike but today this sinner needs a deep clean.
With each step and tear I released every burden I went by each sin one by one this was going to turn into more than a stroll but a journey.
What started as a light rain turns into a tempest reflecting my inner pain my emotions and weather in sync sorry to anyone else who stepped outside today.
The tears fall, my heart beat thunders my crying out strikes like lightening begging to be saved I think I picked the wrong day to come outside.
I think The Almighty can hear his childs reaching out because through the storm clouds the sun begins trying to make it's way through fighting all the hurt and pain of this weary soul.
It's rays reaching for me like a father trying to hug a child I reach back to accept the warmth and as soon

as we touch peace takes over the rain and my tears begin to subside.

I turn my face to His glory letting Him heal my broken spirit and renew my fractured faith. Today I walked outside with no umbrella to let the rain blend with my tears only to find my biggest fear was if Jehovah left me but He showed me that He will always be there to carry me through the storm and the sun will shine on the other side.

Can You?

Can you write me a tune that resonates through my soul invoking my heart to soar through past the moon into heaven greeting Jehovah to tell him I found the one?
Can you create a melody that makes my spirit sing and dance in meadows of purple as the wind sings me your name?
Can you bring out the best of me in harmony and jazz tunes my feet tap at the sound of your breath bird land living in my soul because you love me so?
Can you write the words that fall from my lips dripping lyrics of Nina Simone or Billy Holiday I want to dance all day because your love has me high?
Can you bring my heart to life through strife and pain whisper my name and I will fly like butterflies with no destination lost in your cadence?
Can you soothe my soul with the echoes of rhythm and blues your arms wrapped around me like a cocoon this is home?
Sing a song of praise to our love shout it to Allah outside of the most high you are my comfort zone a place to rest when the world outside is a mess you are my love song.
Can you dance with me make me laugh at our rhythm playful like children in the park carefree and

innocent have others join in our play our love is infectious and care free yes please dance with me?

Can you love me when I'm at my weakest give strength and be my better half as I will try to be yours forever until my last breath?

Can you love me the way that I love you our hourglass never running out this is eternal you are me and I you vows that will never be broken?

Deliverance

You are the dream catcher of my soul the light that shines when I speak your name captor of my heart and King of my castle.

You are the reason I breath and wake each day your embrace is warmer than the sun.

You complete me send me to places beyond this world I seek your utterances to fill empty places in my heart.

You are my comfort zone against a cruel world a place of solace and escape I cherish these moments like a woman thirsting for water.

I breath you in like fresh air as you wipe away my tears I was lost until I found you.

I praise you because in your might there is power unknown to wash away my sinful heart and give me peace beyond measure.

Clarity is what I find when I think of you yearning to hold this moment forever as promised I want to be at the right hand of your mercy.

See me beyond my pain and suffering heal me from within so that your glory shines bright for all to see cradle me in your arms and wash away my years of tears.

In you I find shelter a calm from my inner storm torn between this system of things and your will to guide me to life's waters free.
Find favor in me a sinner from birth struggling amongst the blind make my vision clear take away all obstacles I don't want to fight no more.
I am a refugee trying to find shelter take me in and give me favor forgive me I know not what I do.
I turn it all over to you guide my steps as a lantern and let your footsteps show me the way give me solace please I don't want to hurt anymore.
Give me your peace and I will give you my heart the one most deserving becoming the love of my life.

Happily Ever After

Laughter turns to tears when I see you walk out the door of what used to be our life. No more fun times of laying in bed waking up smiling that the other is still here because now you are fading. With every foot step out, our world crashes at my feet the ringing in my ears sounds like thunderstorms knowing when you close the door it's over . The morning walks enjoying a brand new day together will turn to lonely nights and nightmares when I used to dream of the day we would be in front of the alter speaking our forever. Laughter turns to tears as our love has gone from the sweetest fruits to the most rotten that falls to the ground returning to ash with no mystical Phoenix to rise for here we say our goodbyes. Happily ever after turned into a year and some months playing house emulating a wife with no ring all of the milk for free I should've heeded all of the warnings given to me. Our home now a house with only one key winter is coming and I have no one to cling to but cold sheets and an empty pillow. The laughter you brought to these walls is beginning to fade with every foot step to the door drowning out those happy times . I ask why you must go with tears in your eyes you say you aren't ready but, didn't you know that all the months ago before you slept in my bed and I parted my legs?Did you not know you weren't ready then? When you possessed more than my heart in those passion heated moments it was more than lust but love in it's truest form, did you not know the gift that was being given between heated breathes and passionate kisses? Laughter no longer lingers only my tears as you hand me the keys telling me your leaving to find yourself when I thought we found us when we joined together. After the laughter comes the tears as I say farewell to the one I thought was my happily ever after.

Love Palace

You were the undercurrent of my heart beats a pulse that drove me to that crazy and sad place called love.

My hidden desire a treasure I feared to expose to daylight hours.

Under moonlit nights I fantasized what a world shared only by us would be like.

Would it be all that beautiful running in meadows type shit all hearts and candy land like?

I would soon find it would be none of that. When I presented the key to the beautiful place I built just for you in my heart you said nothing.

Not one word escaped your lips only a look of confusion and a peak over my shoulder at the love palace I created then turned your back on me.

The key still in my trembling fingers I yell for you to come back bewildered as to why you wouldn't want all that my heart could give. Where love once stood rage takes over my love palace turned into a mockery all I see is red and with that I light a match and burn it down to cinders.

The house that my love built lays at my feet turning into a faded memory all dreams shattered and gone past the wind swept away by the torrent of my tears.

The day came when you asked if I was still in love
my cynical laugh actually startled you I laughed and
laughed until the same tears that once broke my
heart were tears of joys at your ignorance.
The moment of clarity you had of realizing all that
could have been at your feet laid out like a feast has
been buried to the depths of the earth never to
return.
Your pain is orgasmic and sublime I love it more
than I could ever love you and in it I find comfort in
a sick distorted way.
I give a toast to you and without a word I say
goodbye to the one who had my heart walking away
though in my mind I say fuck you.

Love Story

I loved you yesterday when we were young and naive hearts still caught up in the newness of we. Young love in bloom springing forth memories that we would reminisce about in our tomorrows. Storms would come and our young hearts couldn't weather the trials and tribulations then but love remained in hidden places.

I love you today once young hearts have become adults going through life separate coming back together completing the puzzle that is us. In our time away loving others taught us how to love each other lessons needed to be a better we.

I love you tomorrow where our future is us resting easy in the park watching our children play or having lazy days sitting in comfortable silence taking it all in that we finally made it to this point. Looking back at our story we will say it was worth every second, minute, hour and year creating our love story.

I love you yesterday.
I love you today.
I love you tomorrow.

Slowly Surely

Slowly surely I walk away from the noise of a broken heart and shattered dreams that promise better days that can never be.

I walk away from lies told through familiar lips on a different person waiting for a change doing things the same evoking insanity.

I walk away from wanting a fantasy yearning for someone real and tangible a love not only spoken but proven in action a satisfaction unrealized but that's what I want.

Slowly but surely I walk away from the faliciy said over and over I deserve better no more excepting the regurgitation said by many of what they can do but no action follows.

I walk away from it all preferring to be alone until I can feel secure beyond words that flutter in the wind lost in translation.

I walk away until I can fall into the arms that will forever hold me in proving that the word love that spills from his lips has meaning. Slowly but surely I walk away from it all until he that is worthy comes. Slowly... Surely... I walk away from.

Bonus Poetry

Am I the Reason

Am I the reason that your heart breaks like a shattered mirror? Pieces thrown against time unretrievable.
Am I the reason that silent tears leave streaks in the quite of night leaving behind unseen scars?
Am I the reason that bitterness has taken over a once loving heart that now beats with the rhythm of scorn?
Am I the reason that your smile has faded into black no longer carrying the shine that I once fell in love with?
Am I the reason that my own heart bleeds for love I can't seem to keep no matter how hard I seek?
Am I the reason that the thing I want the most continues to slip through my fingers even when I think I have a strong grip?
I just need to know... am I the reason?

Black Lives

The cries and demise of black lives blood spilled on concrete killing fields.
Mothers cry as black men are picked off like flies no justice as they rest in peace but, who's picking up the pieces of broken communities policed by crooked cops who's blues hide white sheets?
No justice for peace as the list grows longer a new name added our black girls and boys turned to martyrs.
Another black boy just lost his father for the world to see a memory that will never fade that will be played in court only to find the guilty party innocent.
I guess that one guy Jesse Williams really did have something to say.
Who can be offended now by his speech, but they will find a way to turn a blind eye and not except the truth.
People celebrated the 4th of July as if black people are free lynching ropes turned to bullets open season in full affect.
They want us to trust the police but how can that happen when they kill us so freely?

Iron Sharpens Iron

Like minds give to same thoughts creating a mist of
fulfilling experience.
Writers block broken when iron sharpens iron creativity
sparks a fire.
Ink begins to flow mind goes on overload with words lost
in purgatory.
My paper sings a song happy that I've finally come home
to awaken a spirit that was lost.
It all comes so easy forgot what this release could be
almost better than an orgasm.
Words flow slow and easy like two lovers creating life.
My strife escapes me with each letter that releases a
comfort that is a soothing salve to my soul.
Oh these words how I have missed you and the healing
that you bring.
I am open to your power and embrace this moment like
a Christian getting baptized. Anointed with a gift all I
needed was the right push to reignite a fire deep in my
being.
I am reawakened alive with purpose to give these words
a new life to share with anyone that hears.
I am truly alive with poetry.
Laughter to Tears

VitaGold

The Good Old Days

Whatever happened to real life conversation and actually hearing verbatim you know the times before Facebook and Instagram when conversation was an art and not about likes?
A time when you had to pick up a phone before there was text when remembering a number took effort not just scrolling and pressing send.
What happened to human connection, mental stimulation when talking was needed never passed over for informal emojis and gifs? Technology killed personal contact the way video killed radio too much instant stimulation of unnecessary things feelings expressed behind a computer screen.
You can be whoever you want to be but your true self sending out a representative when reality is shit validation given by followers but who's really behind you in this struggle of life. Will they be there when you send a go fund me then again I guess you need a tragedy to beg for money.
I have been the victim of social acceptance falling into the trap of wanting to be liked when all I ever needed were those truly close to me. Where would be without the need of social media?
People you will never speak to and could care less if you died tomorrow.

Yeah they will say things they may not mean but only joining in so they can be seen. Hashtags and circumstance we all fall into the trap to like or to be liked is now the new question.
Let's figure this out as I post this to social media.

About the Author

Born in Cleveland, raised in New Jersey, JoVita started writing poetry at the young age of 13. It was like a gift given to her to help her through the difficulties of puberty. Writing poetry as "VitaGold" was used to cover the pain and woes of life of a young teenager who was raised by her single-parent father. During this time, poetry became her passion and outlook on life. VitaGold returned back to her home town of Cleveland, Ohio to jump start her career.

In 2010, VitaGold joined the local spoken word scene performing in Cleveland and the surrounding areas. She has performed at several poetry venues like Dreamer's Bar and Grill Writer's Lounge; B Side Lounge; Urban Joe's Cafe - Soulful Expressions; The Stage - Purple Pages and Club 330 located in Akron, OH.

VitaGold's accumen as a writer, a performer and an MC is aptly reflected on her album *Poetic Reflections – The Patterns of Life*.

Poetic Reflections

The Patterns of Life

VitaGold

UPTOWN
MEDIA JOINT VENTURES
PUBLISHING

Sankofa
Freedom Press

www.ingramcontent.com/pod-product-compliance
Lightning Source LLC
Chambersburg PA
CBHW041759040426

42447CB00001B/30